W9-AMU-352

THE
CHRISTMAS
SKY

THE CHRISTMAS SKY

By FRANKLYN M. BRANLEY

Illustrated by STEPHEN FIESER

THOMAS Y. CROWELL · NEW YORK

The Bible tells us that many centuries ago in Judaea, a child was born of Mary, the wife of Joseph. The child was called Jesus.

T he birth of every child is an important event in the lives of the baby's parents, aunts and uncles, and other members of the family. But this birth was especially important. According to the Bible, the event caused great excitement. People came from far away to see the child and bring Him gifts.

There was great joy, for many people believed this child was the long-awaited Messiah of the Jews. They believed that Jesus would show the world the way to peace and brotherhood.

But not everyone felt joyful. Some of the rulers of that time feared that Jesus would become more powerful than they themselves were. In many different ways they tried to destroy Jesus and to persecute the men and women who believed in Him. Finally, Jesus was sentenced to die. Jesus died while He was still a young man, but the lessons He taught during his short life changed the world. Everywhere today, people still study His teachings and try to live by them.

The coming of Jesus, the Christ Child, marked the beginning of Christianity.

For centuries historians, scholars, and religious leaders have tried to find out more about the birth of Jesus. We know only one story of the birth, the one that is told in the Bible. If other stories were written, they do not exist today.

One of the things the Bible tells us is that a star appeared in the heavens at the time of Jesus' birth. The Gospel according to St. Matthew, chapter 2, verses 1 and 2, says:

Now when Jesus was born in Bethlehem of Judaea in the days of Herod the King, behold, there came wise men from the east to Jerusalem,

Saying, Where is he that is born King of the Jews? for we have seen his star in the east, and are come to worship him.

Astronomers have wondered what that star might have been. They, too, want to learn the whole story of Jesus' birth. They have searched through records to discover what the sky was like when Jesus was born.

The star the Wise Men saw must have been an unusual one, for it is not in the sky today. Except for certain new stars (novas) that astronomers can explain, the stars we see today are the same ones that people saw two thousand years ago. Among them there is no star that can be identified as the one the Wise Men saw—the bright star they followed to find the manger in Bethlehem, a town near Jerusalem.

What, then, could this star have been? And where is it now?

Perhaps the "star" was not a star at all. Perhaps it was something else in the sky, something that people thought was a star. In olden days all sorts of objects were thought to be stars of one kind or another.

One kind of object people saw was meteors. These are the streaks of light we see in the sky and still call shooting stars, even though they are not stars. They are made when small bits of material, sometimes as light and feathery as an ash, enter our atmosphere and become very hot. People of long ago did not know what caused meteors. They thought the streaks of light were stars falling out of the sky.

Could the star of the Wise Men, the Star of Bethlehem, have been a shooting star? Could it have been an especially brilliant meteor that streaked across the sky?

This does not seem likely, for meteors are not that rare. Even brilliant ones are seen from time to time. The Magi, as the Wise Men were called, would not have been impressed by a meteor. Most importantly, meteors last only a few seconds; sometimes they come and go so fast you can't be sure you have seen one. But the "star" the Magi saw must have been in the sky for weeks and months, throughout the time that they journeyed to Bethlehem.

Perhaps the "star" was a comet. Long ago, as today, comets appeared from time to time. Comets are part of the solar system: Like planets, they are held in orbit by the attraction of the sun. The tails of comets are wispy, cloudlike formations of gases and cosmic dust that reflect sunlight. Because people did not understand comets, they called them "long-haired stars." The feathery tails reminded them of long, streaming hair.

very now and then comets appear that are bright enough for everyone to see. They may remain visible for several weeks or months.

Could it have been a comet that appeared around the time of the birth of Jesus? A comet might have been visible in the sky throughout the journey of the Magi. People would have seen it and wondered if the long-haired star was a sign of some extraordinary event.

But astronomers think the "star" was not a comet. Astronomers of today can calculate the paths of comets accurately. They know which comets were close enough to Earth to be seen hundreds and even thousands of years ago. And they know there was no bright comet visible around the time when Jesus was born.

If there had been a comet, moreover, chances are that people would not have been happy to see it. They probably would have been afraid. A comet was thought to be a finger of a god pointing toward Earth, warning everyone to beware. Comets were looked upon as signs of disaster; they were "evil stars" associated with famines and floods, earthquakes and disease, and not with joyful events. So it seems unlikely that the Star of Bethlehem could have been a comet.

In 1604, a German astronomer named Johannes Kepler one night saw a star appear where there had been no star. The star grew brighter and brighter with each passing day. It grew so bright that it could be seen in daylight. Then the star faded and rapidly disappeared.

A star that brightens and then fades is called a nova, from the Latin word for new. An especially bright one is called a supernova. Kepler suggested that the Star of Christmas may have been such a star. Surely such a spectacular object would have impressed all who saw it. A nova might have been seen for several weeks, and so could have served as a guide for the Wise Men.

very few hundred years a bright new star, a nova, appears. However, astronomers know that there was none in the sky anywhere near the time that we believe Jesus was born.

There were, however, other starlike objects that could be seen around the time of the birth. These were "wandering stars." Wandering stars are what we now know to be planets. They change position, seeming to wander among the stars. One or more of these wanderers could have been the sign that told the Wise Men the Messiah had been born.

Astronomers know how long it takes planets to go around the sun, so they can figure out the position of each planet in the sky at any time in history. What, then, were the positions of the planets at the time of Jesus' birth?

I t is customary to assume that Jesus was born in the year 1. Our calendar starts with that year, and calls all the time following it A.D., for *anno Domini,* meaning "in the year of our Lord." But a careful study of history leads us to believe that Jesus was born a few years before A.D. 1.

In the first century A.D., a man called Flavius Josephus wrote a history of the Jewish people. In one part of his history Josephus described events that occurred just before the death of King Herod. "Now it happened that during the high priesthood of Matthias, there was another person made high priest for a single day, that very day which the Jews observe as a feast, and that very night there was an eclipse of the moon."

Josephus went on to say that the new high priest was appointed because of the sickness of King Herod the Great, a brief sickness from which the king shortly died. The feast to which Josephus refers was probably Purim, a Jewish religious observance. We are told the feast was held at the time of a lunar eclipse. That gives a clue to the time of Herod's death. Astronomers know there was a partial eclipse of the moon on March 13 in the year now referred to as 4 B.C. (before Christ). It was the only eclipse occurring on or near any religious festival for several years before or after 4 B.C.

herefore, Herod must have died a short time after March 13 in 4 B.C. We know that Herod was king of Jerusalem at the time of Jesus' birth. So Jesus must have been born in the early months of 4 B.C., or sometime earlier than 4 B.C.

The Bible tells us just how much earlier the event might have happened.

Herod had heard of the birth of Jesus. He commanded the Wise Men who were going to the birthplace to come before him in Jerusalem. He asked them to return to him after they had found the child, and tell him exactly where the child was. Then Herod himself could go to worship Him. We read in the Gospel according to St. Matthew, chapter 2, verses 9 and 10:

When they had heard the king, they [the Wise Men] departed; and, lo, the star, which they saw in the east, went before them, till it came and stood over where the young child was.

When they saw the star, they rejoiced with exceeding great joy.

But after seeing the child, the Wise Men did not return to Jerusalem as Herod had ordered. The Bible tells us that in a dream, angels warned them that Herod did not really want to worship Jesus. Rather, Herod planned to destroy Him. So the Wise Men returned to their homes by another route.

erod was angered by their disobedience. Because he was angry, and because he feared this infant child who was called King of the Jews, Herod ordered a brutal murder. We read about it in the Gospel according to St. Matthew, chapter 2, verse 16:

> Then Herod, when he saw that he was mocked of the wise men, was exceeding wroth, and sent forth, and slew all the children that were in Bethlehem, and in all the coasts thereof, from two years old and younger, according to the time which he had diligently inquired of the wise men.

We do not know exactly how long it was from the time when Herod saw the Wise Men until the time when they were expected to return to Jerusalem. It must have been no longer than two years, for Herod, to be sure that Jesus was destroyed, ordered that all children two years old and younger should be slain.

Joseph, too, had been warned of Herod's treachery in a dream, and escaped into Egypt with his family. After a short stay, Joseph brought Mary and their infant son out of Egypt into the land of Israel, for King Herod had died, and so there was little to fear. Herod died in 4 B.C. At the time Jesus must have been no more than two years old. So He must have been born sometime in 5 or 6 B.C.

he Bible gives us another clue that leads us to believe Jesus was born not in A.D. 1, but several years earlier. In chapter 2, verses 1–7, of the Gospel according to St. Luke, we read:

> And it came to pass in those days, that there went out a decree from Caesar Augustus, that all the world should be taxed....
>
> And all went to be taxed, every one into his own city.
>
> And Joseph also went up from Galilee, out of the city of Nazareth, into Judaea, unto the city of David, which is called Bethlehem; (because he was of the house and lineage of David:)
>
> To be taxed with Mary his espoused wife, being great with child.
>
> And so it was, that, while they were there, the days were accomplished that she should be delivered.
>
> And she brought forth her firstborn son, and wrapped him in swaddling clothes, and laid him in a manger; because there was no room for them in the inn.

Two thousand years ago the Roman Empire spread all around the Mediterranean Sea, and every person in the empire had to pay whatever taxes the emperor demanded. During the reign of Caesar Augustus three tax orders were sent out to the people. We know this from writings on a stone tablet uncovered by archaeologists working near Ankara, Turkey, in 1923. This tablet, an inscription from a Roman temple, was a record of many events of the times, and it included three great tax orders. One of these orders was sent out in the year 8 B.C.

For the tax to be levied, each person had to return to the place where she or he had been born so all could be counted, and the tax could be collected. This is why so many people, Joseph and Mary among them, crowded into Judaea and into the small town of Bethlehem, known as the city of David.

You may wonder how this tax order, issued in 8 B.C., strengthens the belief that Jesus was born around 6 B.C., some two years later. In those days there was no quick way of letting people know of the orders made by their rulers, so tax collections were not made everywhere at the same time. Collectors journeyed from village to village, counting the people, charging the taxes, and collecting the money. They took weeks, months, even years to reach the outer boundaries of the empire. People returning to the places where they were born traveled overland by foot; or by donkey if they were fortunate enough to own one. The journey was tedious and long; many months might pass between the time people first heard of the order and their arrival at the cities of their birth. It seems likely it was the tax order of 8 B.C. that caused Mary to be in Bethlehem when her "days were accomplished" and when Jesus was born.

Events around the time of Herod's death, and records of the tax orders of Caesar Augustus, lead to the same conclusion. Jesus was born sometime between 8 B.C. and 4 B.C., probably in the year 6 B.C.

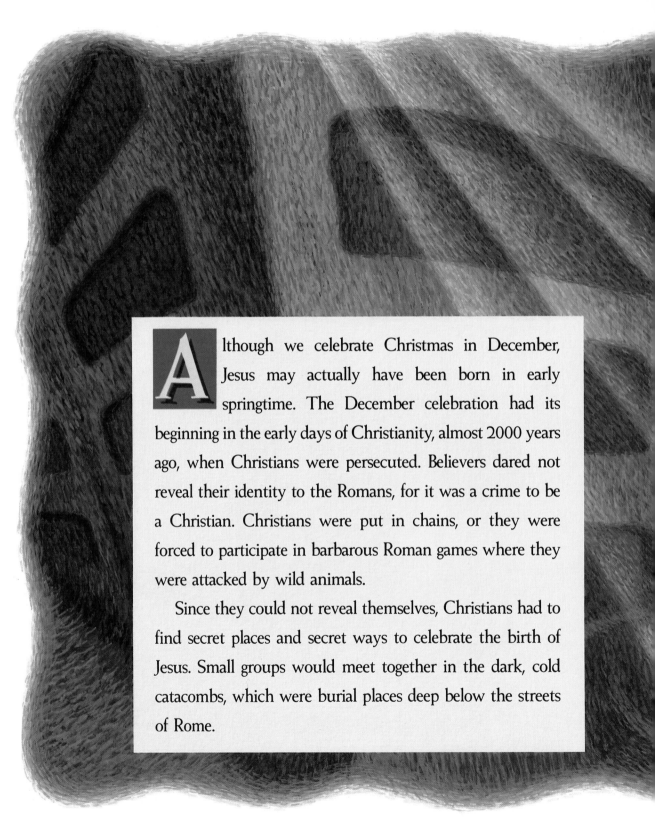

Although we celebrate Christmas in December, Jesus may actually have been born in early springtime. The December celebration had its beginning in the early days of Christianity, almost 2000 years ago, when Christians were persecuted. Believers dared not reveal their identity to the Romans, for it was a crime to be a Christian. Christians were put in chains, or they were forced to participate in barbarous Roman games where they were attacked by wild animals.

Since they could not reveal themselves, Christians had to find secret places and secret ways to celebrate the birth of Jesus. Small groups would meet together in the dark, cold catacombs, which were burial places deep below the streets of Rome.

ut other groups celebrated Christmas on a festival day that came during the Roman holiday period of the Saturnalia. The Saturnalia was a happy time; gifts were exchanged, people danced in the streets, homes were decorated with flowers and the boughs of trees. The climax of the Saturnalia occurred on December 25. Because all Rome was joyful on this day, Christians celebrating the birth of Jesus would not stand out from the crowd.

Long before the Saturnalia was celebrated, since the times of the ancient sun worshippers, December 25 had been an important day. The sun was an important god, one essential to life itself. In summer the sun was high above the horizon, and bathed the countryside with warmth. Crops flourished and there was an abundance of food. As fall and winter approached, the position of the noonday sun became lower and lower. The countryside became bleak and cold. Plants died in the field. There was great alarm that the sun might continue its movement toward the horizon. Suppose it moved lower, and lower, and lower—finally to disappear completely and never to return again? Without the sun, life could not go on. For several days celebrations were held to keep the sun god from leaving the sky. The first day of winter became a time of great joy, for after that day the sun would reach a bit higher in the sky with each passing day.

According to our present calendar, the first day of winter occurs on December 21 or 22. But there have been many different calendars down through the centuries. In the Roman calendar, winter began on December 25 rather than December 21. It was by this calendar that the Saturnalia was celebrated. The noise and excitement of these celebrations, which had started centuries earlier with sun worship, made it possible for some Christians to celebrate the birth of Jesus on December 25.

In the early part of the fourth century, persecution of the Christians ended. At that time, Emperor Constantine, who was himself a Christian, decreed that the birth of Jesus should be celebrated on December 25. This date has since then become the day of celebration of the Nativity in most parts of the world.

The three planets were Mars, Jupiter, and Saturn. Saturn, in the constellation of Pisces, the fish, moved very little. Jupiter moved more rapidly, and Mars was fastest of the three.

As the weeks and months of the fall and winter of 7 B.C. and the early months of 6 B.C. passed by, the planets moved closer and closer together. In the late winter and early spring the planets formed a small triangle in the constellation Pisces.

The Magi knew about the planets. They were astrologers, the astronomers of that time and place. They studied the planets, and they knew of their positions and their motions. They also knew that these three planets were in a constellation where centuries earlier, according to Jewish scholars, planets had appeared around the time of the birth of Moses. Moses was the prophet who was to lead the Israelites out of Egypt to the eastern borders of the Promised Land. Pisces was therefore considered the constellation of the Jews.

The appearance of the planets in Pisces may have been a sign to the Magi that an event of great importance was occurring in the land of the Jews. The Star of Bethlehem might have been these three planets that had moved close together. They may have been the guide that the Wise Men followed to find the manger where Jesus was born.

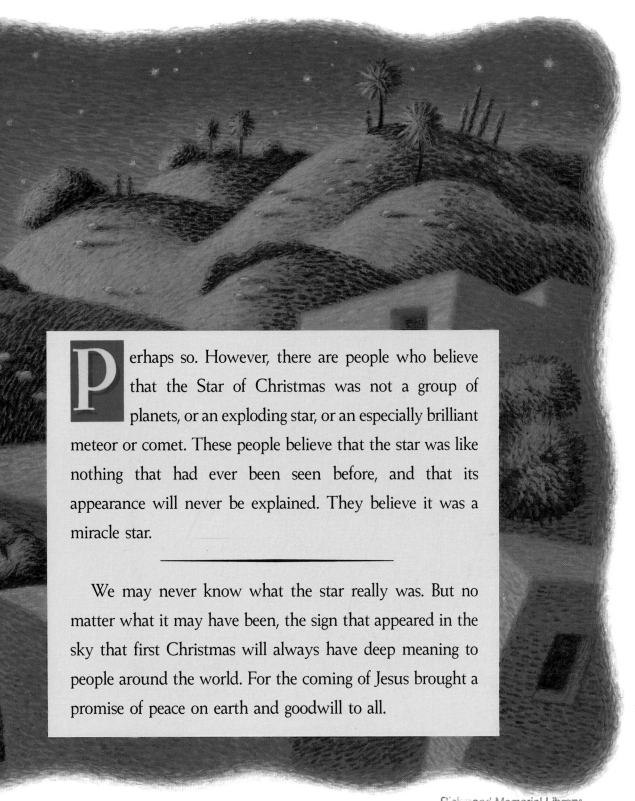

Perhaps so. However, there are people who believe that the Star of Christmas was not a group of planets, or an exploding star, or an especially brilliant meteor or comet. These people believe that the star was like nothing that had ever been seen before, and that its appearance will never be explained. They believe it was a miracle star.

We may never know what the star really was. But no matter what it may have been, the sign that appeared in the sky that first Christmas will always have deep meaning to people around the world. For the coming of Jesus brought a promise of peace on earth and goodwill to all.

Library of Congress Cataloging-in-Publication Data
Branley, Franklyn Mansfield, date
   The Christmas sky / by Franklyn M. Branley ; illustrated by
Stephen Fieser. — Rev. ed.
     p.   cm.
   Summary: An astronomical exploration of the Star of Bethlehem
against a background of the Christmas story.
   ISBN 0-690-04770-3 : $. — ISBN 0-690-04772-X (lib. bdg.)
$
   1. Star of Bethlehem—Juvenile literature. 2. Astronomy in the
Bible—Juvenile literature. 3. Christmas—Juvenile literature.
[1. Star of Bethlehem. 2. Astronomy in the Bible. 3. Christmas.]
I. Fieser, Stephen, ill. II. Title.
QB805.B73   1990   89-71210
232.92'1—dc20   CIP
                                              AC